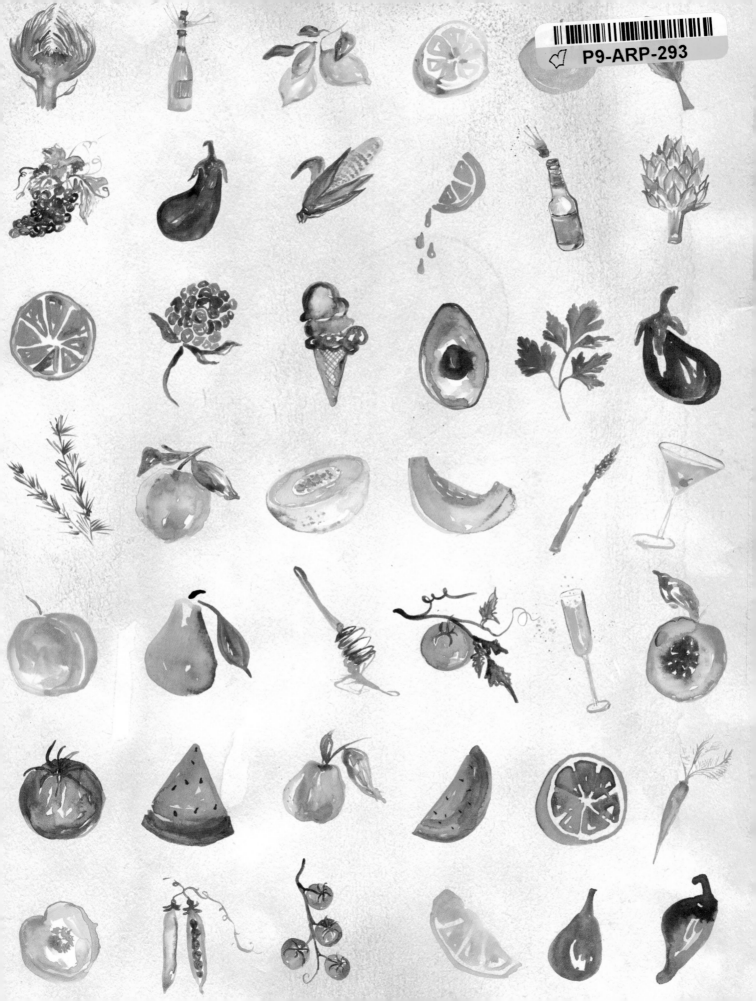

Published in 2014 by Stewart, Tabori & Chang
An imprint of ABRAMS

Library of Congress Control Number: 2013945647

ISBN: 978-1-61769-081-5

Editor: Dervla Kelly
Designer: Erin Gleeson
Production Manager: Tina Cameron

The text of this book was composed in Traveling Typewriter,
Vintage Typewriter, and author's handwriting.

Printed and bound in the United States

10

ABRAMS
THE ART OF BOOKS SINCE 1949
115 West 18th Street
New York, NY 10011
www.abramsbooks.com

for mom & dad

table of contents

introduction

I grew up in an apple orchard in Sonoma County, California, in the 1980s, next door to a minicommune and some goat farmers. We had no TV, we were vegetarian, and we had a huge vegetable garden. Because of the weather, my brother and I were able to spend most of our time outdoors. Our family also spent a lot of time in the kitchen together—in the summers we picked black-berries for pie, and in the fall we made everything imaginable with apples. Years of watercolor classes and dressing friends up for photo shoots in the orchard led me to become an art major in college. I think I really got serious about a career in the arts when I studied abroad in Italy. I got my first "real" camera that year while at the Academy of Fine Arts in Bologna (which is often considered Italy's culinary capital).

Upon graduation, I told my family I was moving to New York to become a photographer. I had no job, a few hundred bucks, and a one-month sublet for a room I found on the Upper West Side through Craigslist. What I thought would be a one-year adventure soon became eight (funny how that happens), and as much as New York challenged me, it rewarded me—oh, how I love that city! While in grad school, I began volunteering as a photographer for the James Beard Foundation, and that was really my entry into the New York food scene. I started shooting food for different publications and books, and got to work with some of the best chefs in the world.

I first met my husband, Jonathan, in 2004 when a friend took me to a party on his roof deck on the Upper West Side. I was instantly smitten, especially when I realized he loved hosting parties as much as I did. Years later when we moved to Brooklyn together, our backyard became a hub for gatherings of family and friends—dinner parties, cocktail parties, costume theme parties, outdoor movie screenings. We hosted constantly, which is where many of these recipes were born. And since I didn't often have much time to prepare, the recipes were ideally quick, easy, affordable, and pretty.

In the summer of 2011, Jonathan accepted a job as a rabbi at a big reform synagogue in Silicon Valley. The thought of leaving New York was devastating for both of us, but it was a great opportunity for him and, in a way, I was ready for a change. Even though I was busy as a freelancer and teaching at The Fashion Institute of Technology, I was exhausted from the hustle to make ends meet and not terribly passionate about any projects I had going. Still, I felt I hadn't yet finished what I'd set out to do by moving.

Sure, I'd had many accomplishments along the way, but there were still so many publications I wanted to shoot for, galleries I wanted to exhibit at, chefs I wanted to meet. In New York, you feel close to the action–like it's all within grasp, and that if you just work a little harder and a little longer, it will happen. Perhaps it's that tangible yearning that keeps people going. As we prepared to leave, I remember saying to Jonathan that I was worried my biggest career successes might be behind me. I just couldn't imagine what my life as an artist would look like if I moved to the suburbs, where I knew no one.

When looking for a place to live in California, we stumbled upon an ad for a cabin in the woods just outside of town, with a separate building I could use as a studio. We knew it would be a complete 180 from living in Brooklyn, but we thought it could be an adventure! The view from the cabin is stunning, but I think what really sold me was the light. There is this glow about the place–a soft golden light that is warm and welcoming, almost magical. It's only miles from the coast, and dramatic banks of fog regularly roll in to create a soft-box in the sky, ideal for photographing outside.

A month after the move, we got married on a ranch near where I grew up, with an outdoor dinner overlooking vineyards at sunset and dancing in a barn. In the weeks following the wedding, while Jonathan was busy with his new job, I found myself alone in the woods unpacking and making art while trying to envision the next phase of my career. It felt daunting to try to re-create a career I'd spent years building in New York. I felt stuck, and on top of it, guilty that I wasn't contributing financially to our household. While I saw the move as an amazing opportunity for reinvention, I had no idea how to get there. I was spending a lot of time on our new deck, looking out onto a canyon of ancient redwoods. I think being around all those trees started to calm and refocus me. There's something about spending hours of one's day in nature that can be so grounding. I spent so much time outdoors as a child; I so vividly remember the smell of the blackberries in late summer and the feel of the fluffy dirt on my bare feet after the orchard had been plowed. These types of little geographic sensory details create a unique understanding of a place, something we overlook, but that's so important, and something that doesn't exist in the same way when in a city. In our new home, I love that I know there is a mossy spot on the side of the house that turns green after the rain and that there are bunnies living under the firewood pile out back. I love the soft feel of feathery green new-growth tips on the redwoods and the smell of the bay tree on my walk to my studio in the morning.

When I started showing my work to San Francisco magazine and cookbook editors, it became increasingly clear that the West Coast sensibility was far removed from my minimalist/slick/well-lit work shot in high-end big-city restaurants. My prospective Bay Area clients wanted less beet foam and more kale chips (if you know what I mean). So I started cooking and shooting, and I started a blog, calling it The Forest Feast, mainly so I'd have a link I could send out to editors. "They want earthy, I can GIVE them earthy!" I thought. Without the structure of editorial assignments, and without the immediate pressure to pay bills, I felt artistically free. I had always painted and cooked, but only for friends and family, never considering it part of my professional work. With nothing to lose, I let myself create imagery without boundaries, which led to incorporating handwriting and watercolor illustrations into my photography, which I'd never done before.

Because I am a self-taught cook, the recipes I set out to make were very simple. We signed up for a CSA membership (Community Supported Agriculture), which meant we got a weekly box full of local, seasonal produce. I try to eat local, sustainable food as much as possible, and CSAs make it so much easier. I started experimenting with whatever came each week and began sharing the recipes on my blog.

In my artwork, I've always been interested in diagrams and showing parts of the whole, so it made sense to me to show the recipes visually: ingredients in one shot, finished dish in another. To my absolute surprise, this made sense to others, and I was so happy to receive e-mails from people who found my blog online and were actually cooking from it! The support from my readers has encouraged me to continue sharing recipes and has ultimately delivered this dream project of a book to me. For this, I am so grateful!

I am drawn to color and shape, so often my dishes will start with that in mind. We could have mashed potatoes, or we could have *purple* mashed potatoes. Adding color makes it just a little more fun! And cutting produce into fun shapes can make things more enjoyable, too, like my Watermelon Salad (page 110). Often it doesn't take much more effort to make food look unique and attractive in addition to tasting good, and my goal is to share some of those simple ideas with you. I want to present recipe ideas that are easy enough for a weeknight, yet impressive enough for a dinner party. My hope is that this book will find a nice balance between your coffee table and your kitchen counter and that you will be inspired to cook, eat, share, and enjoy colorful, healthy food together.

Cheers!

Erin

how to use this book

I love collecting cookbooks, but rarely have time to sit down, read all the directions, and make any of the dishes. Whether it's a weeknight dinner or I am scrambling to get something together for a dinner party, I need a recipe that is quick, healthy, delicious, and colorful. When I look at a recipe, I want to be able to scan the ingredients, see the picture of the finished dish, and have a basic idea of how I could make it. My goal with this book is to present accessible recipes in that way: visually, beautifully, simply.

Colorful produce is the main inspiration for my dishes and I prefer to keep things simple to really highlight the natural flavor. It's amazing what just a little olive oil and salt can bring out in a vegetable! Overall, the recipes have few ingredients, few steps, and I believe they can be made by anyone. I encourage creativity and substitution if you are missing something, and I try to make suggestions along the way for items that may not be available everywhere or year-round. In general, I prefer to leave the peel on most fruits and vegetables, so I leave peeling up to you in recipes that call for things like cucumbers, carrots, beets, pears, plums, and apples.

Though I like to start with local, seasonal produce, I don't claim to be a purist. If I need a tomato for a recipe in the winter, I will buy one. I hope these recipe ideas will be a starting point for you-feel free to be creative with what you have in your cupboard! Although I prefer to make most everything by hand, there are things I don't often have time for (like pesto, pie crust, puff pastry, or gnocchi). If you are able, I encourage you to make them from scratch, but if buying pie dough will mean you'll actually have time to make that galette, why not?

You won't need to make a long shopping list for most of the recipes, plus I use many of the same ingredients repeatedly. Items I like to keep stocked in my kitchen include onions, garlic, garlic powder, Parmesan, puff pastry, Greek yogurt (any percentage is fine), eggs, nuts (pecans, almonds, walnuts), dried fruit (cherries, cranberries, golden raisins), and fresh herbs (especially cilantro and basil). I love cilantro and use it often since it comes year-round in our CSA (as do avocados-oh, California!). When I chop it, I include the stems because they have a lot of flavor (and picking all those little leaves off is tedious!). If you're not a cilantro lover (and I know many aren't), feel free to substitute parsley or basil. Also look for best-quality extra-virgin olive oil, coarse/kosher sea salt, and freshly ground black pepper (these are in almost every recipe). I love Maldon sea salt and use it to top most dishes before serving.

The recipes each generally serve four people, but since many of them could function as either a main or a side, this is just a guideline. Many of my dishes can be served warm or at room temperature, which makes them ideal for entertaining. Although I grew up vegetarian and cook primarily that way, I like the idea that these dishes could easily be served as sides with a non-vegetarian entrée. I do almost all my roasting and baking of vegetables on a large baking sheet with a short rim. I usually keep things on the middle rack and prefer the vegetables to be tender when poked with a fork, but not too overdone. For extra tips on each recipe, please see the notes at the beginning of each chapter.

CUTTING TECHNIQUES

TO CUT A (FIRM, RIPE) AVOCADO INTO ROUNDS:

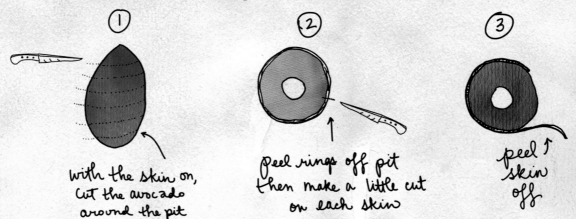

① With the skin on, cut the avocado around the pit

② peel rings off pit then make a little cut on each skin

③ peel skin off

TO CHIFFONADE GREENS & HERBS:

① Stack leaves

② Roll the leaves, then cut thin strips

TO CUT VEGETABLE RIBBONS:

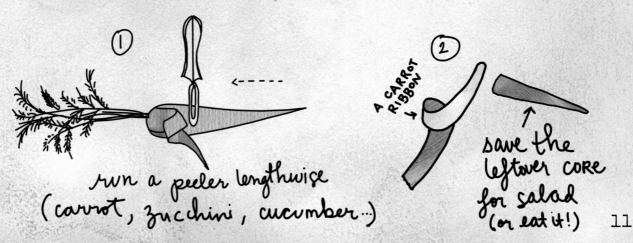

① run a peeler lengthwise (carrot, zucchini, cucumber...)

② A CARROT RIBBON

save the leftover core for salad (or eat it!)

appetizers

Jonathan and I have a joint love of entertaining and many of these recipes that were born at cocktail parties in our backyard in Brooklyn have transitioned to gatherings on our deck in the redwoods. These recipes serve about four people unless otherwise noted and are great paired with one of the cocktails on pages 57–79.

Beer-Battered Artichoke Hearts page 18

Artichoke fields run along the coast near Half Moon Bay just over the hill from us, and these are served at several restaurants there. Try them with one of the dipping sauces on page 88.

Guacamole Deviled Eggs page 20

These are my go-to party food. The avocado replaces some of the yolk, making them a little lighter.

Asparagus Tart page 22

A free-form tart (galette) with egg, cheese, capers, pine nuts, and store-bought puff pastry dough. Can be cut small and served with toothpicks.

Asparagus Pastry Straws page 24

Strips of puff pastry are spiral-wrapped around stalks of asparagus, sprinkled with Parmesan, and baked.

Baked Brie page 26

My family always makes this around the holidays-it's so decadent. The round of cheese is topped with minced garlic and herbs, wrapped in pie crust, and baked. Gooey garlicky goodness! If I have extra dough left-over, I like to make little flowers and decorate the top.

Garlic Knots page 28

I use store-bought pizza dough and roll the knots in butter and fresh garlic. Best eaten hot! Try them sprinkled with herbes de Provence.

Caper-Burrata Crostini page 30

Shallots and capers are fried and then spooned over burrata-covered bread. Burrata is like a creamier fresh mozzarella-it's one of my favorite cheeses. Finish with Maldon sea salt.

Honey-Pepper Fresh Figs page 32

Fresh figs are drizzled with honey, then sprinkled with feta, red pepper flakes, and mint. Sweet, savory, and spicy in one bite.

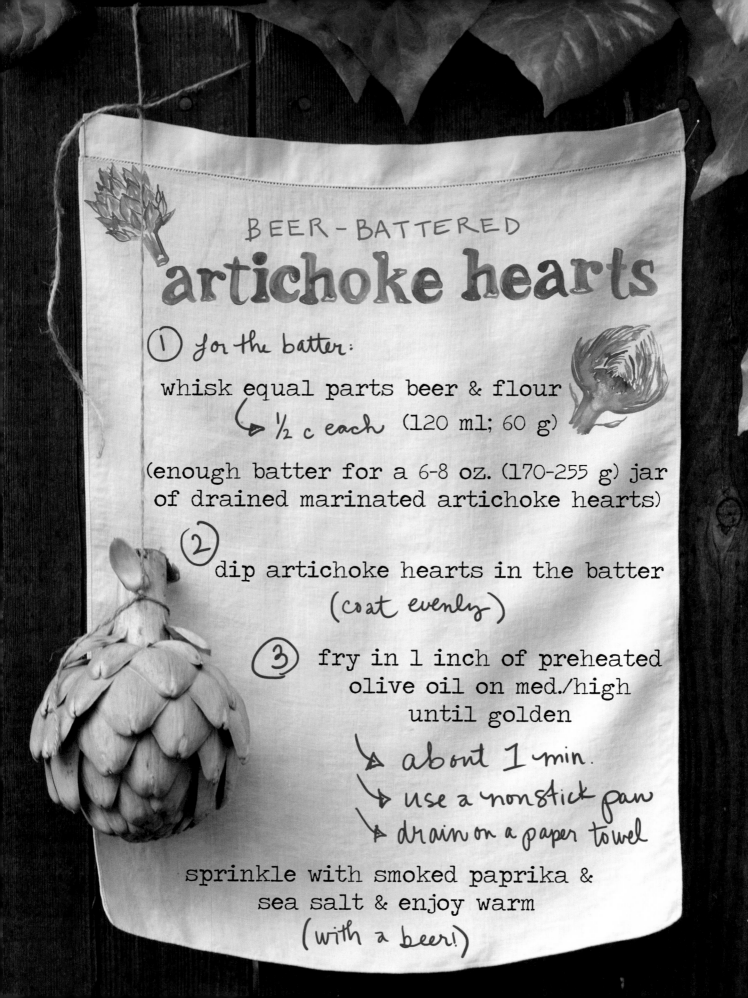

BEER-BATTERED
artichoke hearts

① for the batter:

whisk equal parts beer & flour
↳ ½ c each (120 ml; 60 g)

(enough batter for a 6-8 oz. (170-255 g) jar
of drained marinated artichoke hearts)

② dip artichoke hearts in the batter
(coat evenly)

③ fry in 1 inch of preheated
olive oil on med./high
until golden

↳ about 1 min.
↳ use a nonstick pan
↳ drain on a paper towel

sprinkle with smoked paprika &
sea salt & enjoy warm
(with a beer!)

GUACAMOLE
DEVILED EGGS

① halve 6 peeled hard-boiled eggs & remove yolks

② combine 2 of the yolks (discard others) with 1 ripe avocado, plus:

1 T mayonnaise
1 t spicy mustard
½ t garlic powder
Salt & pepper

③ mash it all together & spoon into egg whites

garnish with →
red pepper flakes

asparagus tart

1. lay out 1 sheet of defrosted puff pastry on a greased pan

(pinch edges up to make a crust)

2. spread a thin layer of soft cheese over the surface (I use Brie)

3. beat an egg & pour it evenly over the cheese layer

4. lay about 15 raw asparagus stalks over egg (ends trimmed)

sprinkle top with {
2 T pine nuts
2 T capers
½ t garlic powder
½ t dried Italian herbs
salt & pepper
}

Bake 375°F for 20 min.
until puffy & golden

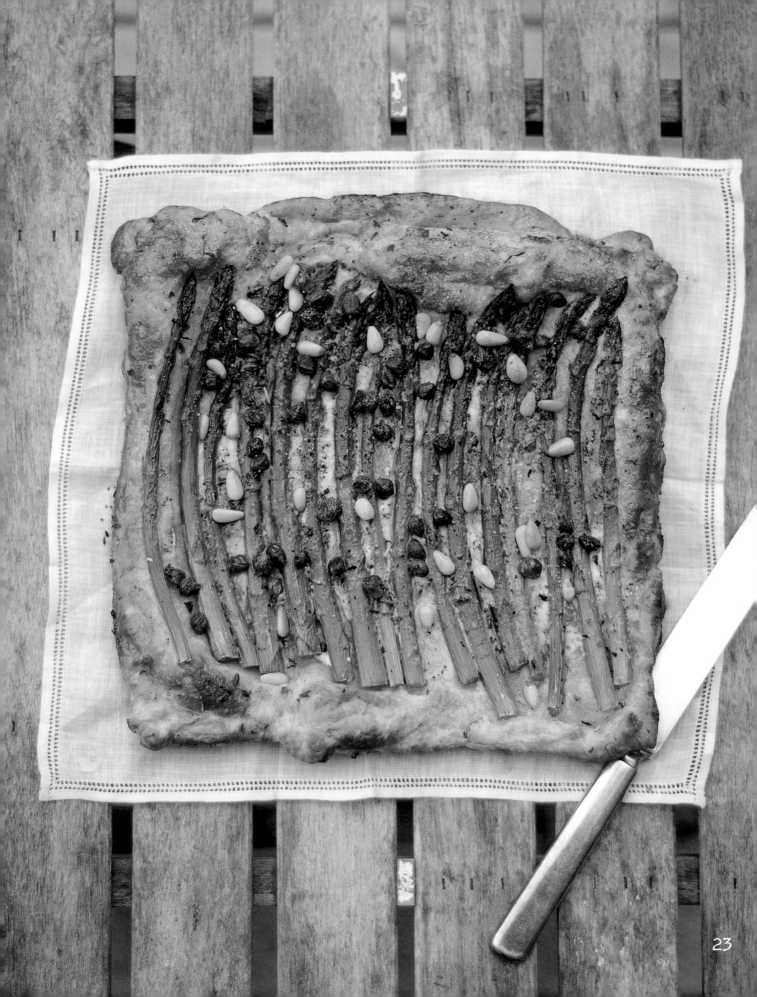

ASPARAGUS
PASTRY STRAWS

① you'll need:

1 bunch of asparagus
(about 30 stalks) & 1 sheet
of puff pastry (2 sheets come
in a 17-oz. or 480-g box)

② cut puff pastry
into ¼-inch strips

③

wrap 1 pastry strip
around each
asparagus stalk

④ arrange on a
greased baking sheet

⑤ then...
sprinkle with
Parmesan, salt, & pepper

Bake at 375°F for 15 min.
or until golden

try them with a dip from page 88

baked brie

if there's excess dough, use it to decorate the top! →

mix {
1 T finely chopped fresh rosemary
6 cloves garlic, minced
1 T chopped fresh parsley
}

spread garlic mixture in the middle of a (premade) 10-inch pie dough, leaving room around edges

place an 8-oz. (225-g) round of Brie on top of the garlic mixture & fold over the edges of dough, pinching to enclose it, then flip it over onto a greased baking sheet

Bake at 375°F for 20 min. or until golden

serve while warm, with slices of baguette

garlic knots

cut an 8-oz. (225-g)
package of
store-bought
pizza dough into
8-inch strips

tie the strips
into knots

bake on an oiled sheet
at 350°F for 15-20 min.
or until golden

melt 2 T butter in a pan with
4 cloves garlic, finely minced

roll the knots in the butter mixture
when they come out of the oven

sprinkle with salt & enjoy immediately

CAPER - BURRATA
CROSTINI

Slice & toast 1 baguette

sauté in 2t butter until soft:

2 minced shallots

1 small (3.5-oz. or 100-g) jar of capers (drained)

put a spoonful of burrata cheese on each slice of bread

plus 1 T caper mixture

sprinkle with salt before serving

apricot bites

top each dried
apricot with:

1 t goat cheese (chèvre)

← rolled into
a little ball

then

1 dried cranberry →

& a sprig of fresh

← thyme

strawberry salsa

1 tomato

¼ c (10 g)
fresh cilantro

1 small carton
(about 2 c or 280 g)
of strawberries

juice from ½ of a lime

¼ of a red onion

finely chop & combine
all with a pinch of salt

SERVE with crackers or chips

french radishes

trim ends off 10 radishes,
then slice them in half

top each radish half
with ½ t room-temp. butter

then sprinkle them
with coarse salt
(like Maldon)

try these with the Skylonda
Cocktail on page 76

polka-dot focaccia

① use the recipe for challah on page 230. don't add the sugar, but do add 2 T chopped rosemary. after dough has risen once, press it into a 10-by-15-inch oiled baking sheet.

② press grapes & cherry tomatoes into dough. Sprinkle with sea salt & let rise 30 min.

③ bake at 350°F for 20-25 min. or until golden

④ serve with olive oil for dipping

gorgonzola grapes

← 1 bunch of grapes

in the palm of your hand,
roll each grape in:

1 t creamy
gorgonzola cheese

↓

then in a bowl of finely
chopped toasted pecans

serve
with
toothpicks

baked garlic nuts

WITH WHOLE GARLIC CLOVES & ROSEMARY

2 heads of garlic
(about 20 peeled cloves)

1 T finely chopped
fresh rosemary

1 c (134 g)
unsalted
raw mixed nuts

① First cook the garlic:

garlic
rosemary
2 t olive oil
¼ t truffle salt
} Mix & roast on a
baking sheet at 350°F
for 15 min. or until
garlic is soft & golden

② Then add the nuts:
mix nuts with garlic mixture on the
baking sheet & roast another 5 min.

transfer to a bowl,
mix, & salt to taste

LEEK
medallions

cut the white part
of 1 leek into
¼-inch circles

* 1 beaten egg
* ½ c bread crumbs
  (60 g)

dip each leek round into
egg first, then bread crumbs

fry in olive oil until golden
* nonstick pan
* about 1 min. each side
* medium heat

drain on paper towels
then salt & serve with
a dip from page 88

parmesan lace

finely
grate →
6 oz. (200 g)
of Parmesan

a pinch
of cayenne
on each pile

drop 1 T piles of cheese
onto a hot pan (med/high)
* use nonstick *

fry 1 min. per side (or until golden)

↳ drain on paper towels

(they get more crisp as they cool)
serve alongside a cheese plate
or on top of a salad

cream cheese-filled

parmesan poppers

for the dough:

beat 3 egg whites
to stiff peaks

then fold in:

1½ c (150 g) →
grated Parmesan

CREAM CHEESE FOR THE FILLING

¼ t cayenne
↘

① flatten 1 T of the dough in your palm
② put 1 t of cream cheese in the center of the dough
③ fold up edges to form a ball, pinch closed
④ heat 2 inches veg. oil on med/high in a nonstick pan
⑤ fry, turning once, until golden & puffy (1 min.)
⑥ remove & drain on a paper towel

enjoy immediately while warm!

51

SAGE
chips

heat ½ inch olive oil
in a small saucepan

↳ on med/high

drop fresh sage leaves into hot
oil until slightly browned

↳ 1 or 2 min. (watch closely!)

remove with a slotted spoon,
cool on a paper towel

↳ sprinkle
with salt

enjoy alone with a cheese plate or on top of soup

↖ kitchen window

my studio ↗

cocktails

We always serve beer and wine at our parties, but it's fun to have one "special" drink to share. A lot of these can be made in a pitcher ahead of time so guests can help themselves. By leaving out the hard alcohol, several of the drinks below can be made as "mocktails."

Cucumber Spritzer   page 60

This refreshing white wine spritzer is served in a glass lined with a pretty cucumber ribbon.

Cherry-Tomato Michelada   page 62

I fell in love with this spicy beer cocktail on a trip to Oaxaca, Mexico. My version has a salt and pepper-rimmed glass and is garnished with cherry tomatoes.

Bloody Mimosa   page 64

Blood oranges come in our CSA all winter and I love mixing their juice with sparkling wine.

Blackberry Negroni   page 66

This drink is typically garnished with orange, but since we have wild blackberry bushes, I use berries as a garnish in the summer instead. The sweetness of the berries brightens up this slightly bitter, refreshing drink.

Blueberry Sparkler   page 68

Frozen blueberries are used instead of ice in this vodka drink.

Lemon-Basil Mojito   page 70

Lemon slices, mint, and basil leaves are frozen into ice cubes in this rum drink.

Rosemary Gin Fizz   page 72

I leave out the traditional egg white and use melted honey instead of simple syrup. Garnish with a sprig of fresh rosemary.

Winter Citrus Sangria page 74

This red wine sangria is packed with the citrus that comes all winter in our CSA box.

The Skylonda Cocktail page 76

This is my favorite cold-weather cocktail! I want to drink it all winter by the fire. It's a warming bourbon drink with cinnamon and orange. It was inspired by the Manhattan and is named after our new neck of the woods. If you don't have time to make the cinnamon bourbon, it's also good with straight bourbon.

Chai Hot Toddy page 78

Chai spices are a warming addition to the usual hot toddy. A cute garnish is created by pushing cloves into a slice of orange. I make it with whiskey, but you could also use brandy or rum.

cucumber
SPRITZER

use a peeler to
make a long cucumber
"ribbon" to line
← a wine glass

add ice to the glass,
then add equal parts

white
wine

seltzer

garnish
with
fresh
mint ↙ ♡

serves 1

CHERRY-TOMATO
michelada

① rub a lemon on the rim of a glass, then dip it in a small plate of salt & pepper (mixed, about 2 t each)

② pour into the glass in this order:

* juice from ½ a lemon
* 3 drops hot sauce
* 1 cold light beer

③ garnish with cherry tomatoes on a mini kebab stick

serves 1

PEPPER

SALT

BLOODY MIMOSA

Squeeze 1 blood orange & pour
juice into a champagne flute

Add 3 drops of bitters

Top it off with
chilled rosè champagne

serves 1

Blueberry Sparkler

¼ c (35 g) frozen blueberries (instead of ice)

3 T vodka

¼ c (60 ml) berry juice (any kind)

top it off with seltzer

garnish with lemon slice

serves 1

LEMON-BASIL mojito

freeze fresh
mint, basil,
& lemon slices
into ice cubes

Muddle
in a glass:

chiffonade { small sprig of basil
small sprig of mint

1 t sugar or honey
1 t lemon juice
3 T rum

add the lemon ice cubes
& top the glass off with seltzer

serves 1

rosemary gin fizz

serves 1

① 3 T gin
1 t melted honey
juice from ½ a lemon } stir well in a glass

② add ice

③ top it off with seltzer

stir & garnish with a fresh sprig of rosemary

the SKYLONDA cocktail

serves 1

for the cinnamon bourbon:
soak 3 cinnamon sticks
in a 12-oz. (360-ml) jar
of bourbon for 3 days

& then
strain

mix:

* 4 T cinnamon bourbon

* 2 T dry vermouth

* 1 t bitters

serve over ice with a slice of orange

•••chai••• hot toddy

stir {
1 c (240 ml) steeped chai tea
3 T bourbon
2 t honey
}

← push whole cloves into an orange slice for garnish

serves 1

salads

These salads could be served as a main attraction for a light meal, or as a side. As you'll notice, few of them are lettuce salads. (I think it might be because I don't like washing lettuce!) But I also like my salads to be more filling and "meaty," so I use more chopped vegetables and sometimes even cooked ingredients as well. All of them can be served at room temperature, which means they are easy to make ahead and keep in the fridge for a weeknight dinner, or when getting ready for a party. When making salads ahead, I recommend dressing them at the last minute. When serving family style, I let each person dress their own so leftovers will stay crisp. I often eat these with just a bit of olive oil, lemon, and salt. But feel free to serve them with one of my dressings on pages 86–89. Each recipe serves 4 unless otherwise noted.

Kale Caesar with polenta croutons   page 90
With a creamy garlicky dressing, pine nuts, and Parmesan.

Beet Salad with Pink Eggs   page 92
Hard-boiled eggs are dyed pink in beet water. Served over a bed of arugula.

Butternut Caprese   page 94
This is one of Jonathan's favorites (and mine, too!). Avocado and roasted squash are added to the usual caprese ingredients.

Potato-Green Bean Salad   page 96

With cilantro and garlic. If you're not a cilantro lover, try it with basil or parsley.

Orange-Cabbage Salad   page 98

Lots of salads are fun when served in a purple cabbage bowl, but this colorful, crunchy combo is a favorite of mine.

Carrot Slaw   page 100
With golden raisins and pecans.

Eggplant Salad   page 102
When traveling in Israel, I fell in love with fried halloumi cheese on top of salads. Since it is not always easy to find, I created a similar recipe using mozzarella. It's best not to use fresh mozzarella here, as it melts more easily.

Lentil Salad   page 104
Canned lentils work great, but if you make your own, boil them like pasta on low to avoid them turning to mush. This filling salad is tossed with sun-dried tomatoes, purple cabbage, cherry tomatoes, and dried cranberries.

dressings MADE IN A *jar*

#1 SESAME-SOY DRESSING

↑ *shake it!*

↑	↑	↑	↑	↑	↑	↑
¾ c (180 ml) olive oil	¼ c (60 ml) rice vinegar	2 t sesame oil	2 t soy sauce	½ t garlic powder	1 T sesame seeds	1 chopped scallion

#2 HONEY-CHIVE DRESSING

SHAKE!

↑	↑	↑	↑
¾ c (180 ml) olive oil	¼ c (60 ml) white balsamic vinegar	1 T honey	2 T finely chopped fresh chives

each recipe makes about 1¼ c (300 ml) dressing, enough for about 4 salads

(#3) CITRUS DRESSING

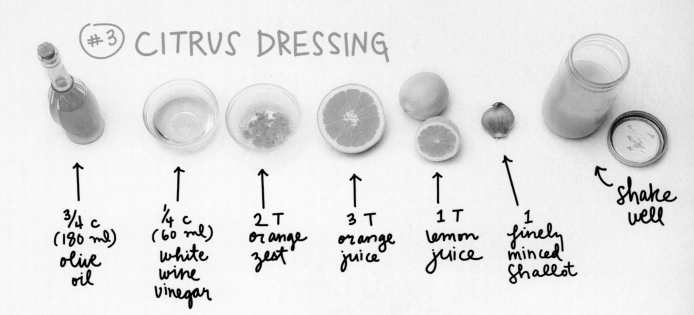

↑ ¾ c (180 ml) olive oil

↑ ¼ c (60 ml) white wine vinegar

↑ 2 T orange zest

↑ 3 T orange juice

↑ 1 T lemon juice

↑ 1 finely minced shallot

↰ shake well

(#4) LEMON-MUSTARD VINAIGRETTE

↑ ¾ c (180 ml) olive oil

↑ ¼ c (60 ml) lemon juice

↑ 2 T Dijon mustard

↑ 1 t maple syrup

↰ shake it, baby!

these keep at least 1 week in the refrigerator;
bring to room temperature before using

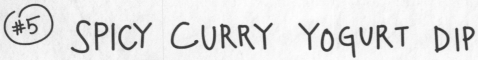

dips YOU CAN stir

(#5) SPICY CURRY YOGURT DIP

1½ c (425 g) plain Greek yogurt

¼ t cayenne pepper

2 t curry powder

1 T lemon juice

Stir well

(#6) HERB-CUCUMBER DIP

1 c (285 g) plain Greek yogurt

½ c (65 g) finely chopped cucumber (I don't peel)

¼ c (10 g) chopped fresh basil

1 T lemon juice

½ t garlic powder

1 minced scallion

STIR

MAKE THESE USING A *blender*

#7 GREEK CAESAR DRESSING

↑ 3/4 c (180 ml) olive oil

↑ 2 whole garlic cloves

↑ 1/4 c (70 g) plain Greek yogurt

↑ 1 T lemon juice

↑ 2 t Dijon mustard

↳ blend well

#8 ARUGULA CHIMICHURRI SAUCE

↑ 3/4 c (180 ml) olive oil

↑ 1/4 c (60 ml) red wine vinegar

↑ 1 c (20 g) arugula

↑ 2 whole garlic cloves

↑ 1/2 t red pepper flakes

↑ 1/4 c (10 g) fresh cilantro

↳ BLEND WELL

kale caesar

WITH POLENTA CROUTONS

slice 1 bunch of flat-leaf kale
(about 10 leaves) into thin strips

chiffonade! →

toss with
3 T Greek Caesar Dressing
(page 89) plus:

½ c (50 g) Parmesan
↙ (grated)

¼ c (14 g) pine nuts
↙

for the croutons...

chop 8 oz. (160 g) of store-bought
polenta into cubes & fry until →
golden in 2 T olive oil (nonstick pan)

beet salad
WITH PINK EGGS

Slice 4 beets into wedges & boil 10 min. (until fork tender, peeling optional)

Blend several cooked wedges (about 1 beet) in a blender with 3 c (720 ml) water

Soak 8 peeled hard-boiled eggs in this "beet water" for 1 hour in the fridge to turn them pink

↳ *then slice eggs in half*

serve beets & eggs over a bed of arugula, top with dressing #3 on page 87

potato-green bean SALAD

① roast about 25 mini potatoes
& 10 peeled garlic cloves at 425°F
for 30 min., or until fork tender

↳ with olive oil,
salt, & pepper

② when cooled, toss with ¾ c (30 g)
chopped fresh cilantro &
1 c (100 g) chopped
fresh raw green beans

↳ dress with:

1 T rice vinegar
1 T olive oil

also great with
dressing #7 on page 89

ORANGE-CABBAGE SALAD

slice 4 carrots
into thin ovals

peel & chop 2 oranges
(blood or regular)

slice 5 radishes
into thin circles

use the outer leaves
of a purple cabbage as
bowls & chop the
inside of the head
for the salad

toss all ingredients
with oil & vinegar or
use dressing #3 on page 87

carrot slaw

5 carrots → grated

½ c (50 g) pecans → chopped

½ c (70 g) golden raisins

DRESS WITH:
{ 2 T olive oil &
1 T lemon juice
pinch of salt

or try dressing #3 on page 87

eggplant salad

① slice 1 large eggplant into ½-inch rounds

② roast on an oiled baking sheet
↳ sprinkle with olive oil & salt
8 min. on each side at 400°F
(until browned)

③ dip 8 thick slices of mozzarella
in 1 beaten egg, then in bread crumbs
↳ fry on med/high in
olive oil until golden
(about 1 min. per side,
drain on paper towels)

④ cut 4 elephant garlic cloves
into paper-thin slices & fry
on med/high heat in olive oil
until golden & crisp (30 sec.)

⑤ Layer on a platter:
• eggplant (cooled)
• cheese & garlic
• 1 c (150 g) cherry tomatoes
• ¼ c (10 g) chopped basil

⑥ dress with olive oil, salt, & pepper

slice in half

lentil salad

2 c (400 g) cooked lentils
　　(any type)

↳ to be quick, use canned.
if from scratch, follow
package instructions.

if using dry red lentils,
they can get mushy easily, so
I cook them on med/low for
15-20 min. until al dente,
then strain like pasta & cool

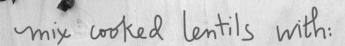
mix cooked lentils with:

½ c (30 g) sun-dried tomatoes
½ c (64 g) dried cranberries
1 c (150 g) halved cherry tomatoes

Spread over 2 c (140g) shredded purple cabbage
dress with oil & vinegar or dressing #4 on page 87

ORANGE-
AVOCADO
...SALAD...

2 oranges
2 firm, ripe avocados
↓
peel & slice into rounds

layer alternating on plate

(avocado peeling technique page 11)

Sprinkle top with:

2 T chopped scallions
2 T chopped fresh cilantro
plus olive oil & salt

nectarine

& TOMATO SALAD

slice into wedges:

{ 3 nectarines
3 tomatoes

↓

on a platter, top with:

{ ¼ c (30 g) crumbled feta
½ thinly sliced red onion
¼ c (30 g) chopped pecans
¼ c (10 g) fresh mint, chiffonade
¼ c (10 g) fresh basil, chiffonade

dress with olive oil & salt

(see chiffonade illustration on page 11)

persimmon
—SALAD—

8 fuyu persimmons

fuyus are the short squat ones that are best raw & firm. remove seeds & cut into chunks (peeling optional)

¾ c (30 g) chopped fresh cilantro

(I include stems; they are flavorful!)

½ of a red onion (diced)

3 scallions (chopped)

seeds from 1 pomegranate

toss all with juice from ½ orange & 1 lime, plus 1 T olive oil & salt

strawberry-cucumber
RIBBON SALAD

make ribbons from 2 large cucumbers using a peeler

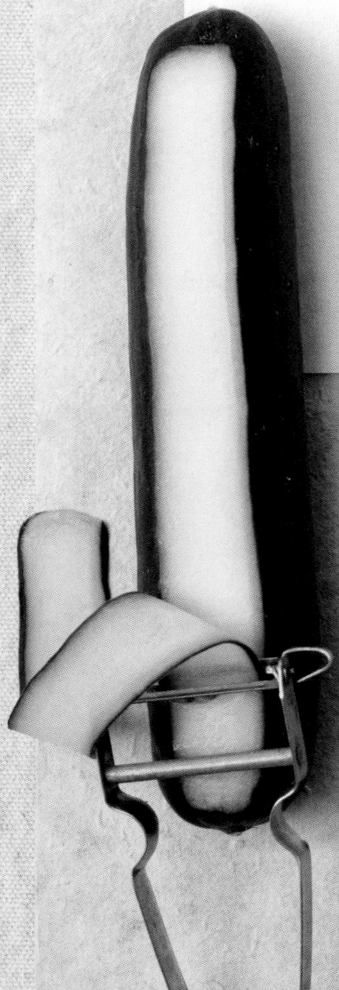

←

Combine with:

{
1 c (170 g) sliced strawberries
½ c (60 g) crumbled goat cheese
¾ c (75 g) sliced snow peas
½ c (45 g) sliced toasted almonds
}

↓

dress with olive oil & lemon juice

salt to taste

watermelon radish SALAD

layer these ingredients on a platter:

← **1 large watermelon radish**
(thinly sliced by hand or with a mandoline.
chop some into matchsticks for garnish)

2 peeled oranges
(sliced into ¼-inch rounds)

½ red onion
(sliced into thin rings)

2 sprigs of mint
(cut in chiffonade,
see page 11)

2 scallions
(chopped)

dress with olive oil & salt

green salad

Chop:

2 scallions
1 small cucumber
1 green pear
2 stalks celery
½ avocado
¼ c (30 g) pistachios
¼ c (10 g) fresh basil

Combine with:

1 c (140 g) shelled
edamame beans

Dress with:

juice of 1 lime,
olive oil, & salt

or try dressing #1 or #2 on page 86

yellow salad

toss these ingredients:

1 yellow bell pepper (cubed)

1 (16-oz. or 450-g) can garbanzo beans, drained

1 c (150 g) yellow cherry tomatoes (halved)

1 raw yellow beet (peeled & thinly sliced)

1 lemon cucumber (scrubbed & sliced)

½ c (70 g) golden raisins

1 t lemon zest

raw kernels from 1 ear corn

use dressing #4 on page 87

red salad

1 red bell pepper
(cubed)

1 bunch radishes
(about 8, chopped)

¼ red onion
(diced)

¼ c (40 g) dried cherries

1 c (150 g) red cherry tomatoes
(sliced in half)

½ c (90 g) fresh
pomegranate seeds

1 red apple
(cubed)

toss everything
with dressing #2 on page 86

vegetable dishes

I like to eat tapas style, so I can sample a variety of different dishes. I consider these vegetable dishes main courses, and often serve three or four of them together as a meal. But they could also be treated as sides and served alongside any entrée. Each recipe serves 4 unless otherwise noted.

Rosemary Skewers

Rosemary sprigs are used instead of kebab sticks to skewer vegetables. If you have access to a rosemary plant, the stems are usually much thicker and easier to thread vegetables on than store-bought sprigs. It sometimes helps to prepoke holes with a wooden skewer to make threading easier. Also be sure to cut vegetables into large pieces so they don't split.

Bay Potatoes

Circles of potatoes and onions are lined up like dominoes in a baking dish. Since we have a bay tree out back, I use fresh bay leaves between the rounds to infuse this dish with flavor, but dried leaves work great, too!

Carrot & Zucchini Ribbon Pasta

A peeler is used to make pastalike ribbons from vegetables that are mixed with actual pasta and a buttery thyme sauce. I like my ratio of ribbons to pasta to be about 1:1. Lighter, but just as satisfying!

Curried Crispy Carrots

I like how these roasted carrot ribbons have both chewy and crispy bits. They'll be crispier if you keep them from overlapping on the baking sheet.

Accordion Zucchini

The squash has little slices in it, stuffed with fresh garlic and baked. I choose small zucchini and serve one per person.

Baked Apple Rings

A sweet and savory dish with caramelized onions and golden raisins.

Crispy Broccoli & Blue

Broccoli is roasted until the edges are brown and crispy, then tossed with pine nuts and crumbled blue cheese.

Aglio, Olio, & Peperoncino Collards

When I lived in Italy in college, my Italian roommates made "aglio, olio, e peperoncino" constantly. It simply means "garlic, olive oil, and red pepper flakes" and is typically made with spaghetti. I have translated it into a vegetable dish, cutting collard greens into long pastalike strips to replace the noodles.

Cauliflower Cheese Steak

This is my bread-free alternative to an open-faced grilled cheese. Slabs of cauliflower are roasted with cheddar and scallions.

Cinnamon Cauliflower   page 150

We make this dish almost weekly at our house! Sesame and cinnamon add bold flavors to this mild vegetable.

Citrus-Beet Stack   page 152

Boiled beet slices are stacked alternately with citrus. Look for citrus and beets that are roughly the same size. It's easy to prepare ahead when entertaining, and is a unique, colorful presentation. Serve several stacks on a platter or individual stacks on small plates.

Strawberry-Arugula Wrap   page 154

Goat cheese, strawberries, and arugula are wrapped in a flour tortilla. Topped with balsamic vinegar and olive oil, these are fun to take to work instead of a sandwich!

Corn & Cauliflower Tacos   page 156

Topped with hot sauce and Greek yogurt. Served in small corn tortillas.

Eggplant "Tacos"   page 158

Little rounds of eggplant replace the tortilla and are filled with Brie and cilantro.

Roasted Veggie Gnocchi   page 160

This is my go-to dinner when we get home late, and one of my favorite recipes in this book. I roast the vegetables ahead of time. Upon arrival I can cook the gnocchi in just a few minutes and toss it all together.

Baked Kale Egg Cups   page 162

Ramekins are lined with a leaf of curly kale, then filled with an herbed egg mixture and baked. The edges get crispy like kale chips. These are great when making brunch for several people because you can bake a tray of them all at once. Be sure to grease your ramekins for easier cleanup, or use a nonstick muffin tin.

Avocado Egg-in-a-Hole   page 164

Eggs are baked right into the cavity of half an avocado. I suggest propping the avocado halves up in muffin tins when baking to keep the egg from spilling over. Serve with toast!

Sweet Potato Latkes   page 166

We make latkes for Hanukkah every year and this is my favorite variation on the traditional potato pancakes.

Lentil & Butternut Lettuce Cups   page 168

With a lentil, onion, and butternut squash filling.

Spicy Feta Lettuce Wraps   page 170

With feta, avocado, cucumber, and spicy oil.

Purple Mashed Potatoes   page 172

Greek yogurt is used instead of milk or butter to add creamy richness. You can certainly make this recipe with regular potatoes as well, but the purple ones make the dish a little more fun.

Mashed Beets   page 174

A lighter, more colorful alternative to mashed potatoes, with sweet potatoes and apple.

Polenta Portobellos   page 176

Creamy goat cheese polenta is poured into big mushroom caps and topped with caramelized shaved Brussels sprouts and onions.

Quinoa-Pecan Frittata Muffins   page 178

This is a great way to use leftover quinoa! These include shredded zucchini and egg, with a crunchy pecan topping. I make a batch of these in mini muffin tins and grab them for breakfast on the go. Use any color quinoa and follow the package's instructions for cooking. This recipe makes about 12 mini muffins or 4-6 regular-size ones. (Tip: They are also tasty with a dab of cream cheese baked into the middle!)

Red Roasted Carrots   page 180

This is one of the most popular recipes from my blog. I have had readers tell me they have put it into their regular dinner rotation! This same spice blend can also be used on other vegetables.

Roasted Cabbage with cherries & Pecans   page 182

Roasted until the edges are crispy and tossed with dried cherries and pecans.

Scallion Quiche   page 184

Baked with cherry tomatoes and a puff pastry crust, this is great for a brunch or breakfast on the go. You can also add cheese to make it richer. Sometimes I cut it into small cubes and serve it with toothpicks at a party.

Squash Blossom Pizza   page 186

A garlicky ricotta mixture is the base of this white pizza. I use a store-bought 16-oz. (455-g) pizza dough, but you could certainly make your own. The inner stamens of the zucchini squash blossoms can be bitter, so I prefer to remove them. I get the blossoms at the farmers' market in the early summer, but if you can't find them you can just top the pizza with thin slices of zucchini.

Butternut-Pear Soup   page 188

The squash and pears are roasted together then pureed with Greek yogurt and spices. I use an immersion blender, but you can also do it in 2 batches in a regular blender. Popcorn is sprinkled on top instead of croutons.

Sweet Potato-Stuffed Tomatoes   page 190

Tomato halves are filled with mashed garlic sweet potatoes, baked, and topped with Parmesan. You can save the discarded tomato seeds and tops for a tomato sauce.

Warm Cheesy Wheat Berries   page 192

This risotto-like dish satisfies my craving for mac and cheese, and is served with caramelized onions on top. Wheat berries are like a fatter, chewier rice, similar to farro. There are different types of wheat berries, so follow your package's instructions on how to best cook them.

Yellow Squash Galette   page 194

Store-bought puff pastry is topped with pesto, ricotta, and circles of summer squash. This is great warm or at room temperature.

ROSEMARY SKEWERS

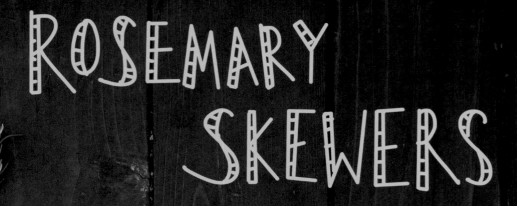

cut in 2-inch cubes

{ 2 red bell peppers
2 red onions

thread peppers & onions onto about 8 rosemary sprigs

(you may need to peel some of the needles off)

drizzle with olive oil, salt, & pepper

Roast at 425°F about 15-20min., until tender (or BBQ!)

bay potatoes

cut into ¼-inch slices:
(try to find potatoes & onions
with a similar diameter)

BAY

serves 6-8

3 sweet
potatoes

3 small
red onions

3 red
potatoes

line up the slices in a greased 9-by-13-inch pan
↳ alternating, like dominoes

slip in bay leaves between every few slices
↳ about 15 dry or 10 fresh (cut in half)

drizzle 2 T melted butter & 3 T olive oil over all
↳ plus salt, pepper, & 2 minced garlic cloves

bake until fork tender & a bit crispy on the edges
↳ 425°F, about 1 hour

135

carrot & zucchini ribbon pasta

Sauté in a big skillet:
(Med. heat, 5 min.)

* 5 garlic cloves (minced)
* ribbons from 2 carrots
* ribbons from 2 zucchini
* 1 T olive oil
* salt & pepper

Then add:

* 8 oz. (225 g) dry fettuccine, cooked

* 1 T chopped fresh thyme leaves

* 1 T butter (allow to melt)

Mix well & serve hot

CURRIED
crispy carrots

① use a peeler
to make ribbons
from 4 large carrots
(see how-to on page 11)

trim ends

② in a bowl, mix
carrot strips with:

3 T olive oil
½ t coarse salt
½ t curry powder

③ bake on an oiled sheet
30 min. at 325°F until edges are crispy

accordion zucchini

① make little cuts all the way down a small zucchini about ¾ of the way through

② slice a garlic clove into paper-thin circles & slip them into the slots

③ drizzle each with: olive oil, salt, & pepper

bake at 375°F for 45-50 min., or until tender

④ sprinkle with about 2 t grated Parmesan 5 min. before it comes out of the oven

CRISPY
**broccoli
& blue**

① **ROAST**
florets from 1 big
head of broccoli
drizzled with
2 T olive oil
until a bit crispy

450° F
20-25 min.

② toss cooked
broccoli
with:

toasted pine nuts &
crumbled blue cheese
(¼ c or 30 g each)

serve sprinkled with olive oil, lemon, & salt
(warm or room temp.)

AGLIO, OLIO, & PEPERONCINO
COLLARDS
(garlic, oil, & red pepper flakes)

remove stems & chiffonade
1 bunch of collard greens
(about 6 leaves)

Combine in a skillet:

2 cloves garlic (minced)
½ t red pepper flakes
2 T olive oil

↳ heat 1 min. on med.
  ↳ then add collards

cook greens 3 min.
until bright green &
slightly wilted

salt to taste

CAULIFLOWER
cheese
steak

Slice a head of cauliflower into ¾-inch "steaks"

<u>roast</u> the steaks on an oiled sheet
375°F for 15 min. per side

(until fork tender & golden)

Top each steak

with 3 T grated Cheddar
cheese & 2 T chopped scallions
plus salt & pepper

Roast 3 more min. or until cheese melts

CINNAMON
CAULIFLOWER

① spread florets from 1 head of cauliflower out on a baking sheet & sprinkle with:

↓

cinnamon
paprika
cayenne
garlic powder
coarse salt
} ½ t each

plus: {
1 t sesame oil
3 T olive oil
}

 ② roast at 450°F for 20-25 min. or until golden, fork tender, & crispy on the edges

citrus-beet stack

Slice 2 large beets into ¼-inch circles & boil 10 min. or until fork tender *(peel if you wish; I don't bother)*

Peel & Slice { 2 oranges
2 grapefruit
into ¼-inch circles

Stack the beet & citrus rounds (alternating), with the biggest ones on the bottom

use dressing #3 on page 87

makes 4 stacks

strawberry-
ARUGULA WRAP

spread 2 T soft goat cheese
on a 10-inch flour tortilla
(I use whole wheat) →

lay out about
5 sliced strawberries
then top those with
¼ c (10 g) arugula

drizzle
before
rolling
it up
{ olive oil →
balsamic ↘
salt & pepper

serves 1

CORN & CAULIFLOWER TACOS

chopped cauliflower
1 small head

corn kernels
2 ears

Roast corn & cauliflower with:

½ t red pepper flakes
½ t chili powder
½ t garlic powder
olive oil, salt, & pepper

425°F, 15-20 min.
(until golden)

spoon into warm tortillas
(enough for 4-5)

top each taco with:

1 T Greek yogurt
1 T feta
hot sauce

eggplant "tacos"

① slice an eggplant into ½-inch rounds

② roast on an oiled baking sheet
↳ sprinkle with olive oil & salt

8 min. each side at 400°F
(or until golden)

③ place a piece of Brie & fresh cilantro
or basil on each eggplant round

fold like a mini taco!

BAKED
kale egg
CUPS

① line a greased 3-inch ramekin with a small piece of curly kale

② pour 2 eggs into the ramekin (beaten or not)

③ *Top with:*
1 T grated cheese
½ t dried herbs
salt & pepper
(mix these in if beating egg)

Bake at 350°F for 20 min.
↳ *or until desired egg hardness*

serves 1

avocado
egg-in-a-hole

① cut 1 avocado in half, remove pit

② place halves face up on a
muffin tin so they won't tip over

③ pour beaten egg into each hole

↳ **1 egg fills 2 halves**

④ sprinkle with grated cheese,
garlic powder, salt, & pepper

Bake

375°F, 15-20 min.

↓

*or until
desired egg
hardness*

*tip:

if pit is small, scoop out a
bit of avocado to make hole deeper before adding egg

SWEET POTATO
latkes
(potato pancakes)

Grate 2 sweet potatoes (I don't bother peeling)

Combine with {
4 beaten eggs
1 clove minced garlic
1 T bread crumbs
salt & pepper

Fry 3 T heaps (forming patties) in a generous amount of olive oil until golden brown
↳ about 3 min. each side on med/high
remove & drain on paper towels

Serve with a dollop of Greek yogurt & a sprinkle of chopped scallions

LENTIL & BUTTERNUT
LETTUCE CUPS

Peel & finely cube

1 butternut squash

dice

1 red onion

sautè squash & onions in
2 T olive oil, salt, & pepper until
fork tender (about 8 min. on med.)

mix with :

2 c (400 g) cooked lentils

*Spoon mixture
into butter lettuce leaves*

SPICY FETA
LETTUCE WRAPS

peel leaves off 1 head
of butter lettuce
(about 8 leaves)

fill each
leaf with:

1 T feta

3 cucumber
spears

2 avocado
slices

dressing:
3 T olive oil
1 t red pepper flakes
pinch of salt
↓
enough
for 8 wraps

purple mashed potatoes

cube 6 purple potatoes
& boil 15-20 min.
(until fork tender)
↳ Peeling optional

drain, then mash with:
- ½ c (140 g) Greek yogurt
- 2 T olive oil
- ½ t garlic powder
- salt & pepper

garnish with butter
& chopped scallions

serve immediately

MASHED BEETS

peel & cube 3 beets, 1 sweet potato, & 1 apple

↳ *roast*
with olive oil & salt at 450°F for 30 min.
(*or until fork tender*)

Mash with:
2 T butter or olive oil
⅓ c (95 g) Greek yogurt
salt & pepper to taste

garnish with:
chopped scallions,
dried cherries,
olive oil, & sea salt

polenta portobellos

① Sprinkle 4 large portobellos with:

minced garlic (1 clove each),
olive oil, salt, & pepper

Bake at 375° F
for 20 min.

② slice paper thin { 8 Brussels sprouts
1 red onion

↳ caramelize these over med. heat
on the stovetop with 1 T butter,
about 15 min. or until golden

③ make polenta on the stovetop:

boil 2 c (480 ml) water, add ½ c (78 g) cornmeal,
reduce to a low simmer, stirring often, until creamy,
about 15 min., then stir in ¼ c (56 g) chevrè goat cheese,
plus salt, & pepper to taste

④ fill caps with polenta & top with onion mixture

Quinoa-Pecan
frittata muffins

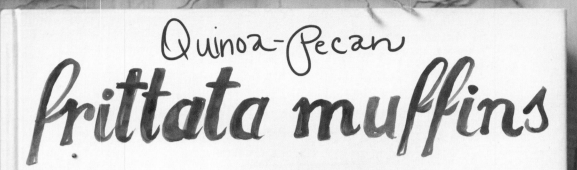

¼ c (45 g) dry quinoa, cooked
(about ¾ c or 135 g cooked)

1 zucchini
(grated)

2 eggs

½ t salt
¼ t pepper
½ t garlic powder
⅓ c (40 g) crumbled feta

mix all ingredients,
then spoon into greased muffin tins
(or use paper liners)

sprinkle each top with 2 t chopped pecans

Bake at 350°F for 20-25 min.
(until egg is firm)

makes 4-6 muffins

RED ROASTED CARROTS

Slice 6 medium carrots diagonally (into ovals)

Shake carrots in a plastic bag with:

½ t each {
cinnamon
paprika
cayenne
garlic powder
coarse salt

↓

plus:

1 t sesame oil
1½ T olive oil

Roast at 425°F for 20-25 min. or until tender with crispy edges

ROASTED CABBAGE

WITH CHERRIES & PECANS

cut 1 head of purple
cabbage into small
wedges (2-3 inches)

spread the cabbage wedges
out on an oiled baking sheet

Sprinkle with:

½ t smoked paprika
½ t garlic powder
3 t olive oil
salt & pepper

Roast:

450°F for 25-30 min.
flipping once,
until edges are crispy

Garnish:

½ c (80 g) dried cherries
½ c (55 g) chopped roasted pecans

scallion quiche

lay out a defrosted sheet of puff pastry in a greased 8-by-8-inch dish

combine & pour over pastry {
6 beaten eggs
¼ c (60 ml) milk or cream
½ t garlic powder
2 chopped scallions
salt & pepper

drop in a handful (½ c or 75 g) of whole cherry tomatoes & lay a few whole scallions over the top

Bake at 375° F for 30–35 min.
(or until set)

squash blossom pizza

① Roll out a 16 oz. (455 g) pizza dough, lay on oiled sheet

② Mix in a bowl:

1 c (250 g) ricotta
2 garlic cloves
¼ c (25 g) Parmesan
1 t fresh thyme
1 t fresh rosemary

③ spread ricotta mixture on the dough & top with 8 blossoms, plus 1 T olive oil & salt

CHOP

MINCE

GRATE

Bake
425°F for 15-20 min.

butternut pear soup

1 butternut squash (peeled)
4 ripe pears (cored)
1 large onion

Cube + Roast
375° F for 30-35 min.
(with olive oil & salt)
until fork tender

↓

pureé with:

4 c (960 ml) vegetable broth
½ c (140 g) Greek yogurt
½ t curry powder
½ t cinnamon
½ t ground ginger
½ t nutmeg

Blend in batches, then
simmer all for 10 min.

top each bowl with popcorn!   serves 6

SWEET POTATO—
stuffed tomatoes

peel, cube, & boil
1 large sweet potato
& 4 cloves garlic
20 min., or until soft

↓

Mash with:

* ¼ c (55 g) cream cheese
* salt & pepper

until nice & smooth

cut tops off 4 or 5 raw
tomatoes & scoop them out
(discard tops & seeds) ↗

Fill tomatoes with potato mixture
(about ¼ c or 60 g per tomato)

Sprinkle
with grated
Parmesan
before
serving

Bake at 350°F for 15 min.,
until thoroughly warmed

WARM CHEESY
WHEAT BERRIES
topped with caramelized onions

3 c (300 g) cooked wheat berries
(see package instructions but
1.5 c or 150 g dry grain &
5 c or 1.2 L water or broth
should simmer 30 min. &
yield about 3 c or 300 g)

for the caramelized onions:

* 1 large onion (cut into thin circles)
* 3 cloves garlic (minced)
* 2 t olive oil
* 2 t butter
* salt

↓

sautè on
med./low 30 min.
or until golden
(stir occasionally)

while hot, mix the cooked
wheat berries with
¾ c (75 g) grated Parmesan

top with the onions
& serve hot

berry picking nearby in Pescadero, CA

sweets

No matter how big the meal, I am one of those people who always has room for dessert. On the average weeknight, I usually just have a piece of chocolate after dinner. But if we're having company, I like to make a little something special. Most of these recipes can be made ahead, so they are ideal for entertaining. Several of these could also work for breakfast or when hosting a brunch party. Recipes serve 4 unless otherwise noted.

Rosemary Shortbread page 202

I love the mix of savory and sweet in this buttery shortbread. I make one big "cookie" in a pie tin and cut it into wedges.

Peanut Butter-Coconut Balls page 204

These no-bake treats are not super sweet, so they are a good snack on the go!

Dates with Orange & Pistachio page 206

Filled with goat cheese and topped with orange zest and pistachios. You can also use cream cheese. These are easy to make ahead and could also work as an appetizer. For a prettier presentation, I use a plastic bag with the corner snipped off to pipe the room-temperature cheese into the dates.

Melon "Cake" page 208

Big circles of watermelon, cantaloupe, and honeydew are stacked to look like a little cake. The inner cavity is filled with Greek yogurt, honey, and almonds. This is fun if you're hosting a brunch.

Dipped Strawberries page 210

Berries are dipped in Greek yogurt, then in brown sugar. That's it! I grew up on these, except we used sour cream instead of Greek yogurt. I like to serve the items in separate bowls so guests can do the dipping themselves.

Greek Parfaits page 212

Greek yogurt is layered in a little cup with fresh raspberries, pistachios, and honey. Use a clear cup so you can see the pretty layers! Topped with a drizzle of olive oil. (This is also great for breakfast!)

Whole Apricot Hand Pies page 214

An apricot is sliced in half, stuffed with butter, cinnamon, and sugar, and then the entire fruit is wrapped in pie crust and baked. I buy the pie crusts that come rolled in a long box (not the kind pressed into a tin). You can use this same method for any stone fruit. The pie will be sweeter if the fruit is very ripe. Served with ice cream and honey.

Fried Banana Split page 216

Served with ice cream and honey.

Apple & Honey Galette   page 218

We made a lot of apple pies growing up in the orchard, and this is a simpler version that just requires two apples. I often make this in the fall on Rosh Hashanah, the Jewish New Year, since it's traditional to eat apples and honey to sweeten the new year.

Plum-Thyme Sundae   page 220

Wild plum trees are surprisingly rampant in our woods, and this is a delicious way to use them up. I serve this sauce warm over vanilla ice cream. I love the tart/sweet combo.

Ice Cream Sandwiches   page 222

Chocolate ice cream and peanut butter layered between soft (store-bought) gingerbread cookies.

Beer Float   page 224

A chocolatey stout is poured over chocolate ice cream and topped with nuts.

Chocolate Ricotta Mousse Cups   page 226

Ricotta cheese is blended in a food processor with melted chocolate, a bit of cinnamon, and brown sugar. This quick "mousse" can easily be made ahead for a dinner party and stored in little cups in the fridge. I prefer dark chocolate, but you can just as easily use milk chocolate.

Peanut Butter-Avocado Shake   page 228

With bananas and almond milk. So creamy and frothy! It could also work for breakfast.

Challah   page 230

If you've never made bread, this slightly sweet braided loaf is a good place to start. I learned how to six-strand braid on Youtube, but a simple three-strand is also lovely. This Jewish bread is typically eaten on Friday evenings for Shabbat dinner. The recipe is not hard, but does require a bit of time. This version is a little sweeter, denser, and cakier than other recipes, which also makes it great for French toast. You can mix things into the dough before baking, like raisins, nuts, or chocolate chips, too! I make a round version of this loaf on the Jewish New Year (Rosh Hashanah) and mix pomegranate seeds in. Be sure your yeast hasn't expired and, in the winter, if your house is cold, turn on your oven, just for a minute; then turn it off and let the dough rise in there.

rosemary shortbread

⅓ c (65 g) sugar

1 c (125 g) all-purpose flour

2 t chopped fresh rosemary

1 stick (4 oz. or 115 g) salted butter

cold & cut
into chunks

PULSE everything in a food processer

↳ briefly! just until combined

press the crumbly mix into a 9-inch round pie tin

Bake at 325° F for 30 min.
or until golden on the edges,
Cool 5 min. before cutting

PEANUT BUTTER-
coconut
Balls

(no bake!)

½ c (125 g)
peanut butter →

10 pitted
dates

1 c (90 g) shredded coconut
plus ½ c (45 g) for rolling

1 T
honey

① Blend
everything in
a food processor
until smooth

② Roll
dough into 2 T balls,
then in coconut

MELON "CAKE"

① cut both ends off each melon to make 4-inch center slices

(save the ends for fruit salad!)

② remove seeds, then stack the 3 centers

③ use a big knife to shave the rind off the 3 stacked rounds at once, cutting down the sides of the "cake" while turning

④ fill the center cavity with ¾ c (215·g) Greek yogurt, then top the stack with:
  ½ c (140 g) Greek yogurt
  ¼ c (22 g) sliced almonds

CANTALOUPE

HONEYDEW

WATERMELON

dipped
strawberries

* 1 small carton strawberries
(fresh, about 2 cups or 280 g)

* ¾ c (215 g) Greek yogurt

* ½ c (110 g) loosely
packed brown sugar

dip each strawberry

FIRST in yogurt →
THEN in sugar
↓

enjoy
immediately

GREEK parfaits

In a small clear glass, using ½ c (140g) Greek yogurt, make alternating layers with:

3 T sliced dried figs →

¼ c (35 g) fresh raspberries →

2 T chopped pecans →

2 T chopped pistachios →

← 2 T honey

drizzle 1 t olive oil on top before serving

WHOLE apricot hand pies

GARNISH WITH CRÈME FRAÎCHE & CINNAMON

①
slice 4 apricots in half & remove pits

②

put ½ t butter, 1 t brown sugar, & a pinch of cinnamon inside each of the 2 halves, then put them back together

③

roll out a 14-oz. (400-g; 9-inch) store-bought pie crust & cut four 6-inch circles; wrap each whole apricot in a circle of dough, pinching edges to enclose fully

④

place apricots pinch side down on a baking sheet

fried banana split

serves 1

cut a banana lengthwise
& fry it face down in
1 t butter for 3-5 min. or
until golden (med. heat)

Arrange on a
Plate & top with:

1 T chopped pecans →

¼ t cinnamon →

2 t honey →

a couple scoops
of ice cream
(about ½ c or 70 g)

APPLE & HONEY GALETTE

lay out a
14-oz.
(400-g; 9-inch)
store-bought
pie dough
on a baking sheet
& top with:

½ c (120g) Brie
1 T brown sugar
3 T sliced almonds
½ t cinnamon

then...

cover the cheese layer with 2 thinly sliced apples

fanned out, peeling optional ✓

dot the top with butter, drizzle with honey,
then pinch the edges to form a crust

Bake at 350°F for 20-25min, until golden;
garnish with pomegranate seeds

plum-thyme SUNDAE

1 t butter

1½ T chopped
fresh thyme →

4 plums, cubed
(I don't bother peeling)

1 T sugar

Simmer everything
on med/low for about 10 min.,
stirring occasionally, until
plums fall apart & become
jamlike (but still chunky)

Cool a few min., then pour warm
heaping spoonfuls over vanilla ice cream

Beer Float

serves 1

pour ½ c (120 ml) dark beer (a chocolatey stout!)

over a ¼ c (35 g) scoop of chocolate ice cream

garnish with 2 t sliced almonds

chocolate ricotta mousse cups

melt 4 oz. (115 g) chocolate
in a metal bowl over
a pot of boiling water
(about 1 bar)

(DARK OR MILK)

½ t cinnamon

1 T brown sugar

2 c (500 g)
ricotta

*blend everything in a food processor for 30 sec,
then spoon into four 3-inch cups & chill 1 hour*

before serving, top with whipped
cream & chocolate shavings

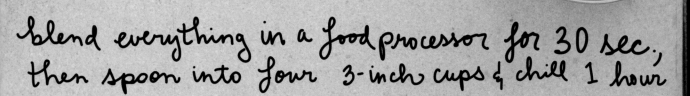

I use a peeler to make shavings

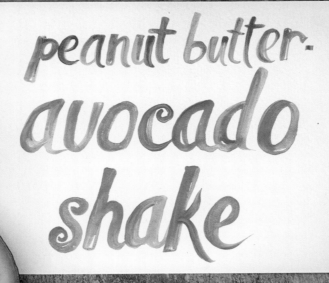

peanut butter·
avocado
shake

½ ripe avocado

1¼ c (300 ml)
milk
(I use almond)

2 frozen bananas
(peel & cut in chunks
before freezing)

3 ice
cubes

2 T peanut
butter

combine all ingredients in a blender until smooth!

serves 2

CHALLAH

(holla!) makes 1 loaf

in an electric mixer bowl (or any big bowl, if by hand)...

mix:

1 packet active yeast (1 T)
¾ c (180 ml) warm water } stir & let sit 5 min. or until slightly bubbly

then mix in:

⅓ c (75 g) packed brown sugar, 2 T honey,
1 egg, 1 t salt, ¼ c (60 ml) veg. oil

continue mixing:

add 3 to 4 c (375 to 500 g) all-purpose flour, little by little, until it forms a ball that is not too sticky

put this ball in a big oiled
bowl in a warm spot &
cover with plastic wrap
until doubled in size

(3-5 hrs.)

next...

braid the dough,
place on an oiled sheet,
brush with beaten egg,
sprinkle with sesame seeds,
& let rise again until puffy
(about 30-60 min.)

Bake

25-30 min. at 350°F
or until golden

Acknowledgments

I am so grateful to have such a warm and supportive family. Even when I was struggling in New York and trying so hard to "become an artist" (a.k.a. interning for free while babysitting, dog walking, and working in a restaurant) they always encouraged me to keep at it. My parents, especially, wanted me to end up with a career that I was passionate about and that made me happy. This book has done just that, so thank you! It's really been a dream project.

To my husband, Jonathan, thank you for giving me the time and space when we first moved to California to find the new direction I needed. That time was pivotal for me because of your love, support, and encouragement. I feel so lucky to be with someone who values the importance of artmaking so highly. Thank you for your patience, pushes when I needed them, constant insight, endless recipe ideas, and honesty while taste testing. Thank you for being my biggest fan—I am certainly yours.

Thank you to my entire family, Jonathan's family, and to all our friends. Thank you for supporting me, cheering me on, and spending countless hours recipe testing. I loved having you be part of this process.

To my rock star of an agent, Alison Fargis, thank you for envisioning this book after seeing my blog and for encouraging me to follow my gut.

To my amazing editor, Dervla Kelly, thank you for discovering my blog and sharing it with Alison. Thank you for giving me the creative freedom to make this project mine, and the guidance to make it so much better. Thank you to everyone at STC for helping me create this beautiful book.

To Anna Rosales, my kind and talented studio/kitchen assistant and "accountabilibuddy." I am eternally grateful that you gave so much of your time to this project.

The making of this book would not have happened without guidance, support, and inspiration from Stephanie Gleeson, Michael Gleeson, Ryan Gleeson, Adam Kotok, Alan Neigher, Kayoko Akabori, Gabrielle Langholtz, Samantha Hahn, Marisa Dobson, Liam Flanagan, Danny Maloney, John and Laney Harney, and Daniel Kosaka.

Last, but not least, thank you to the readers of The Forest Feast blog. Your sweet notes keep me motivated to continue sharing recipes, and your support from the beginning was essential to bringing about this book.

Index

THE WALDORF - ASTORIA

PARK AVENUE AT FIFTIETH STREET, NEW YORK 22, N.Y.